# The Pagan Rain

Poems by

STEVE HOLT

Copyright © 2024 Steve Holt
All rights reserved
First Edition

Fulton Books
Meadville, PA

Published by Fulton Books 2024

ISBN 979-8-89221-664-7 (paperback)
ISBN 979-8-89221-665-4 (digital)

Printed in the United States of America

For Linda, my beloved and dependable leaning post.
And for Tim and Marlene Hanner, splendid friends.

All praise to the hawk on fire in hawk-eyed dusk be sung.
—Dylan Thomas

There is a magnificent violence hidden in a raindrop.
—Loren Eiseley

# Contents

Acknowledgment .................................................................... ix
Critical Thinking .................................................................... 1
The Pagan Rain ...................................................................... 2
Salut! ....................................................................................... 3
A Lesson on the Blue Ridge ................................................ 4
Owen's Home ........................................................................ 5
Argonne Forest: November 1914 ........................................ 6
Separations ............................................................................. 7
The Different Ashes .............................................................. 8
The Staining ........................................................................... 9
Hard by the Susquehanna .................................................. 12
Sundays on Camargo Knob ............................................... 14
Lifting Off the River ........................................................... 15
Allegheny Mountain Aire ................................................... 16
Gun Rites .............................................................................. 17
The Ten Thousand Years ................................................... 18
The Cycle .............................................................................. 19
Crossing Old Fields: A Meditation .................................. 20
As I Lay Lightly .................................................................. 24
Among Lilacs ....................................................................... 25
Stopping Along a High Road in Quebec ........................ 26
In the Greenbrier Valley .................................................... 27
Under a Frugal Summer Sky ............................................. 28
Sylvan Spell .......................................................................... 29

| | |
|---|---|
| The Long Climb | 30 |
| Natural Selection | 31 |
| In Passing | 32 |
| Labor of Love | 33 |
| The Fire by Night | 34 |
| Old Times | 35 |
| The Cold Doldrums | 36 |
| At the Grotto on St. Mary's Mount | 37 |
| I Have Been Thinking of Late | 38 |
| John Chapman: His Vision | 39 |
| The Primitive | 40 |
| Sounding Loon Mountain: Circa 1890 | 42 |
| A Peaceful Day in the Natural World | 44 |
| A Reckoning | 45 |
| Praise | 46 |
| John Proctor Speaks Privately on All Saints' Eve | 47 |
| The Railyard in December | 48 |
| One Small Hour in Autumn | 49 |
| Ninth Month | 51 |
| Existential Exercise | 52 |
| Go Down in Darkness | 53 |

# Acknowledgment

Thanks to my friend Robin Clay for her assistance in preparation of this manuscript and for her magnanimity.

# *Critical Thinking*

Of late, time intimates to me
I have lived as a book of verse,
Born on page 3, following
Two leaves of foreknowledge;
And then a poem for every page,
A page for every year. Just a few,
To date, have bothered to read
Some small part of my oeuvre;
Or I theirs, for that matter,
Over coffee in the ease of cafes
Or beer in the dark wood of pubs
Where we prate about in an effort
To identify our underlying themes.

# The Pagan Rain

The pagan rain on Catoctin Mountain

Penetrates a hood of trees

Shocks and batters rocks

Chills the wild underbrush

Unclothes fall's flowers

Dives like rousing thought

Into frothy shudders of current

And joins the mad chatter of chutes

Before calming

To the loose ends of desire

In waters of gold-cupped leaves

Fit to waft an autumnal newborn

Goddess toward an iced aged shore.

# *Salut!*

> Among the blossoms, a single jar of wine.
> No one else here, I ladle it out myself.
>                             —Li Po

Alone in the moonlit silence
I think on my drunken comrades

Who gathered every evening
And loafed around the pool table

Inside the one-pump gas station:
Boys who one by one passed early

In our time. I pour the wine of dark
Berries raised in rough thickets

And plucked from prickly vines,
And I lift my cup in a slant of praise.

# A Lesson on the Blue Ridge

Early mornings out of misted trees
came green Acteon, stylish as a stag hound,
through damp grass to the back steps
of a chink-logged bed-and-breakfast.

Guests hand-fed the soft-shoe yearling
who accepted the grain and ate
like royalty dining in a hunting lodge.
Till the time came when Acteon failed

To appear from the forest, nor did he
ever again. Such is what comes from loving
a creature bound to grow and pursue
the salt-spring lure of the wilderness.

# *Owen's Home*

So young leading his command
On a makeshift bridge across the Sambre Canal
(Yet another man-made trench)

Wilfred Owen was shot through his skull and died:
One of more than nine million bees perishing
in the smoking hive that was Europe in the 1910s.

And no diaphanous humming, of course,
can come from the most brilliant corpse.

Seven days pass till news of the peace
rings out from cast-iron bells and all
across the browning greensward of Oswestry:

Owen's home.
Let the bittersweet tolling be his last poem.

# Argonne Forest: November 1914

Among the rugged
And ripped trees
In the dead silence
Of suffering ceased;
Of ground gashed
And stones run red;
Of bone-bared wood
Lands scorched sterile;
Of jaw-dropped heads
Of still raw boys;
Of sounds so fiery
That tongues charred;
And of limbs frozen
In gesture futile,
A shepherd wind
Herds down the sky
Flock upon ghost-
Sheep flock
Perfect in design,
Of crystalline flakes
Falling in a freeze
Of white solitude

Hiding, for a time,
Both the scarred
And the shattered
Things on earth.

# *Separations*

Consider the tree as ancient
Sign of womankind, flowering
The ten million centuries.

Consider then all the mothers
Who must watch their ten thousand
Beautiful offspring mature

And leave home every fall windborne
And scattered on the rise and decline
Of stone-strewn paths and wagon ruts.

# The Different Ashes

Under the sun of a chill noon wind
Drifted leaves from a line of blue ash
Settled on the last green grass
In a churchyard by the riverbend.

The rector came out of a heavy door
And his soul was moved: The north wind
Soon would come carrying its baggage:
Lonely colors paling the floodplain;
Ravages of larkspur by bloodthirsty frost;
Slaps and stings from storms of sleet;
Snowblind slides on icepack curves;
The crack-snap-crash of maple bones;
Silences weird and cruel as knife stabs;
Dim-lit days no longer than a swansong.

The rector spent the morning raking decay
Into a pyre; he set it afire, offering up
The dead in ghostly smoke from white ashes.

# *The Staining*

Of "the animal Christ was rumored to have died for."
—Robinson Jeffers

    Loaded stems of cattails at creekside
    Stir in the shallows like brushes
    Straining to filter the evening air.
    Over a sagging corrode of barn roof
    And across fields of dim decline
    Flies a bronzing band of grackles,
    Their yellow searchlight eyes hunting
    Nature's latest dross. Darkness comes
    Soon, sooner now.

    In the barn Laban Marks catches Leah
    Unaware, snatches her by the hair
    And splays her, pins her face-down
    Over two stacked bales of hay. A bucket
    Of water she has pumped for the horse
    Spills down into the dirt. "Don't scream,
    Don't! Goddamn it, don't you scream!"

He gutters, thinking, "Now I've got her
Broke down like a gun barrel." Boring
And grinding in ambush, he ignites
An awful fire inside her: hymeneal flow
Racked with newfound shoots of pain.

The red proof of her ravaged font flows.
She smells a stench of bib-overall grime,
Cheesy layers of sweat, the stink of mud
And muck, manure on gumboots.
A massive shag of head hangs over her,
Unloads moonshine's flagrant breath.
Choking in a hay-wisp swirl she thinks,
"O father, my father!" and low crawls
Into the cave of primal nothingness.

Rising in his stall, the nacre-maned stallion
Slashes at the gate and drives it open.
His eyes throw flames to set the barn ablaze
As he attacks the attacker, snorting
The fury of some equine guard fighting
In an ancient mountain pass. Rearing
High, he crushes white bone of skull,
Scatters grey matter of brain. Far off
The morning train runs screaming
Past the fresh plowed fields of labor.

(The preceding stanza results mainly
From this poet's fruitless musings;
The horse never escaped his stall, not at all.
Rather, once the assault ran its course
The hard old man hitched up a gallus
And trod the trail of dust back to the house.
And Leah? Once she fetched her strength
She too returned to that clapboard shell,
Averting her eyes as she passed
Her mother, who bent over a wash pan
Snapping a new mess of beans;
Laban beat time in his hickory rocker
As if swinging to and fro, to and fro
From some atavistic tangle of vine.
In her garret room, Leah changed
Into her washed-out cotton dress
Worn and forlorn. She was late to school.)

# Hard by the Susquehanna

Behold a surfeit of dark ground
Gained from native bones of old

Ground into the stones of an age;
Paths of hunters crossing native

Names rarely sung, meaning
Less and less in holy valleys

Now gleaned by humble spirit.
Now all plow all sweat all yield

All praise in isolate bliss of Old
World in new. Bread of hearth

Scent wafts across stable farm stables.
Glisten and gloss of rainfall,

Windfall of apple peach plum:
Gems polished and gathered.

Out of barns in dayshine
Manes shine in play, high-blown

Hooves down pastures crackle;
Wild geese whirr, chant

Shape notes through fog-lift
Off grain-gold to garner; green

Waves slide over blue river
Stones sun-glazed in autumn

Shallow hurried current.
It is good, it is now

Wither the stones of an age
And the native bones of old?

## *Sundays on Camargo Knob*

Among stones sown vertical
In an early country graveyard
A trio of Guernseys, calm
As morning's music, graze
In high meadow grass and low
Under a young sun high-
Lighting a royal crown of dew.
Wise creatures, nodding praise
To the rounded order of days.

## Lifting Off the River

I stood today in a fall field
Of corn stubble low and dry.
Twenty-two wild geese, in light

Winged mystic whirr, passed sky—
Drawn toward a rarefied bond
To an ancient urgent order.

And came their native shout,
A bold blue shout about
Some far-flung respite, their course

Wind-strung and saintly. They rose
And rose rhythmic
From unseen springboards of air.

And I, knowing I had missed
Another evolutionary flight,
Stood fixed as a figure in wax.

# Allegheny Mountain Aire

Couched in stone
And roughriding wild
Currents quickened by spring's
Fledgling wings,
Youghiogheny headwaters shout
Raucous, shout joyous
To thaw, fall, and flow
Flow, fall, and thaw
Old ice and snow
Down off the wispy heights
Of time and on,
Breaking up the ice
Floes that stall hibernal man
Till like the snow
Bird out in the bracing cold
He sings for life
And the love that drives it.

# Gun Rites

Seen one cold autumn morning beside a supermarket pump:

Tossed alongside an all-terrain vehicle
A deer lies limp and stretched in the bed
Of an extended-cab, four-wheel-drive pickup.
Its head hangs low over the tailgate.
Beside the eye-dulled creature: Its slayer,
Armed and tricked out in camouflage,
Salutes a crowd gathered in a spellbinding
Mix of spilled gasoline and spilled blood.
He recounts his feat with words that leap
Foul as dung from his boisterous tongue.

The van from Channel 12 News has yet to arrive on the scene.

# The Ten Thousand Years

In the valley we bow and plow the cornfield.
The sun, he is the goldsmith
Who works the shining filigree we gather.

In the valley we bow and plow the wheatfield.
The sun, he is the practiced house chef
Who prepares the fruits of the seed we scatter.

The moon, she is a clay jar brimful and frothed.
We drink deep and slip into cool night dreams
Once removed from the creative frenzy of the sun.

# The Cycle

In a March of mud I think
On the tracing of old forms

The phallic ploughshare
The fecund loam

The penetration
The vectored planting

The underworld descended
The dark dank time

The blessing of water and sun
The faith and anticipation

The sown, it is risen!
The warm yield renewed

The slow death in the garden
The saving of the seed

The ceremony of fire
The spreading of ashes

The circle come full
The satisfaction

# *Crossing Old Fields: A Meditation*

---

I.
The blood flow of history
prefers to be recorded
in the cursive style,
punctuated by memory.

II.
Once I, a boy in his ease,
crossed iron-red fields

to a high bluff above
a laggard creek

emptying itself
into a shore-shaping

ever river named Oyo
by Shawnee to the north.

III.
The bank below, slogged
in a sudsy swirl of slough,
offered a baffle of mushroom
creeping up through clusters
of swamp mallow. Rushes
had broken through a pane
of reptilian amnion
and grown like earth's own
grizzled beard. Primordial
scents of sex and decay
floated in a smother of air,
and mosquitoes sang
fevered praises to boglands.

IV.
A great stone obelisk
stood on the upper bank
like a beacon tower,

massive enough that
only a team of oxen
could have hauled it

two hundred miles from Fort Pitt
through the wilderness.
Its fanciful capstone lay

toppled and broken
from siege after rough siege
by the warriors of weather.

On its face, inside a wreath
of ivy leaves in bas-relief,
faded chiselings showed:

Isham Shreve, 1795–1797
Caledonia Shreve, 1793–1797
Mary Boyce, 1741–1798
John Shreve II, 1797–1800
Rebecca Shreve, 1775–1800

*They died in the arms
of their Savior.*

Few clues thereabout
to define those people's
existence. No grand house's

crumbled foundation
remained, nor shard
of evidence of barn

either rotted or burned.
No well long dry,
no diminished rock wall.

V.
I heard a sudden singing
from a tangle of bramble bush
wrapped in ivy darkly.

It was a slight and dusky thrush.

Sunning at the base of the tomb
a quickening struck out
toward the thick mystery of brush.

I read the deft sculpting,
of his uncurl and flourish
as he wrote in his classic script.

The bright birdsong hushed.

VI.
Thinking down the decades
I now know I caught once
the febrile breath
of a century hard as flint

but chipping away
and fighting outside its time
a frontier death.

# As I Lay Lightly

As I lay lightly, high
above my hospital bed, consciousness
began a slowly floating exit. Enter
A dark-robed prince
in his stealthy stage socks, reciting
for me a silvery soliloquy. It was
lovely, it was
sad as an invitational hymn.

And gladly would I have applauded
those dreamy lines
had not dawn come and ushered in
the bright torchlight of day,
unmasking the false player
who quickly bowed and fled the scene.

# Among Lilacs

All the loosened lilac blossoms paint
On uneasy wind a watercolor purple

And I think of Walt Whitman, shocking
With a love both tender and manly.

And then I think of you, kinsman,
Beautiful kinsman moody and troubled.

Of you, who also came into this world
Ahead of your time

And left it awfully
Long before your time.

## Stopping Along a High Road in Quebec

Sleet assaults the stones of an old-style wayside inn.
Through a stronghold door we slip the bluster of northern spring.
Woodsmen and watermen break fasts and speak plain
the refresh of morning.
We sit caught up in another language
we hardly comprehend.
Coffee pours down like black rain.
Bread comes browned from a baked clay oven; served
under butter-and-maple drizzle it is sweet
to the tongue, rustic and genuine as the sounds of the locals.

# *In the Greenbrier Valley*

The passenger train hurtles along
Beside the swift-water-falling stream.

Its owlish headlamp probing
The mountain dark. Its startling song

Tightens the loosened strings of night,
Its sound resounds ghostly past

Staid stone and a symphony of trees.
Inside the coaches sit still small riders

Swept on by the motion of power
Plowing an urgent furrow of steel.

# *Under a Frugal Summer Sky*

Beneath a dusty shade of undergrowth,
Cross-legged on the cool dirt he sits.
Stained poplin work shirt. Striped railroader's cap.

In his lap an eight-pack of doughnuts,
Powdered. Slowly he chews, slowly swallows.
He smiles in his overall ease. He feels safe.

Down the road, she squints from a cinder-block stoop,
Her eyes on fire, shaded by heavy hands. Over
An hour ago she sent that man to the store.

# Sylvan Spell

Let us go and enter a wood
of blue-green music and honey
suckle tangles of promise.

Let us tread ground studded
with ancestral poplars rooted
under mosses and held fast.

Let us gather wild grapes heady
as the mythic fruit of Bacchus
and dark as the earth below us.

Ah, love, let us love! And let the saintly lark
unseen in the leaves above
sing praises to this holy order.

# The Long Climb

No more will she run wolflike
Baying an instinctual blood chant
With the berserker pack, ripping

Through silver fields and high grass.
She scents a coming blue wind now,
Its green promise soft and mossy.

Ah! she has crossed the rippling creek
And climbed the grey stone slope
With pads worn and claws dulled

Until she has found low-flamed
A hunter's fire on the far hilltop.
She curls and feels ease bone-deep

As she blinks great hazel eyes
And hears the final horn blast
Fading down the last long valley.

# Natural Selection

This spring a piercing red-tailed hawk
Has commandeered Sawmill Hollow,
Greened-up and thick nowadays
With underbrush and vine twine.

Patient as the hourglass of old time
He grips his lookout, a dead limb
Above a cattailed pond, till
He suddens into gear and dips,
Rips and decapitates some
Unsung thing.
And no sweet flute trills
Fill the shrill sounds of his war song.
In mythic darkness was this wingman
Designed to fly missions of blood,
And the only grace he ever needs
Shines in the beauty of his flight.

# *In Passing*

The wind shakes
the painted dust off
the brief butterfly's wing
rustles the fur
from the hickory leaf
bends the browning grass

Leaf butterfly grass
you and I
love
the wind
time
never again
the same

# Labor of Love

Oh! Look dear! The inmates
From the county jail
Are on work detail
Planting poppy seeds
To beautify
The courthouse lawn.

# The Fire by Night

In 1924 and under cloaks of darkness, a torchlight parade of mummers convened in a schoolyard worn hard by hard soles in times of mud and dust. Flashing bravado born of pistol, of bunting knife, of rope, they marched in mad procession: It was a masquerade in white. From two felled locusts an unsteady cross was cobbled and set aflame with a flare. Bootleg whiskey circled 'round the circle of devotees. Stiff-necked righteousness, mixed with biblical harangue reived from context, held sway. No voice of protest or reason sounded. The hour passed; buckets of water scalded the dying fire. The weak chain of beings broke apart, each man striking out for home in bitter frost, dragging his fear of the brother behind him.

# *Old Times*

Since the local steel mill's flaming
Breath went out of blast, its furnaces
Lie in slow and quiet corrode.

Dried flakes of red rust peel and fall
Like scales of long-slain dragons.
Now the men who worked there

Gather mornings at the same table
And pour out their shortened story
As steaming coffee grows bitterly cold.

# The Cold Doldrums

Inside a shanty at the north end of the railyard
an old head took the floor:
"For fourteen months of the war, I headed up
a platoon stationed in Iceland.
Winds blowing heavy snow hard.
Fjords icy and deep.
Nights that lasted all day and all night.
A few hours'd go by, and we'd have to take cover
again from enemy planes overhead, gunning
bullets through the ice pellets.
Pressure, constant pressure is what it was.
And boys, a total of thirty-two American GIs
couldn't stand it anymore.
Took their own lives."
He paused, spat, adjusted his work cap.
"And then one of the men in my own outfit
climbed onto his bunk and pulled a wool
blanket over his head, rammed the barrel
of a .45 into his mouth, and fired.
That made thirty-three.

Next morning the commanding general
sent out an order, 'From this time forward
no more suicides shall be allowed on this island.'
But boys, that turned out not to be the solution."

# At the Grotto on St. Mary's Mount

Out of gravid clouds fall
Rain is falling (cold glass beads fall)
A sacred mountain stream falls
(Water blessed by water)
Past purple aster, purple silkweed
Past chicory blue as sainthood.
Leaves (port-wine-red like bloodstain)
In small wind whirls spiral and wing
And pass (all things planted decline
And fall in autumn) yet one perfect fruit
Was born of an unstained womb once.
And though frost-touch and deep-freeze
Lessen and deaden to winter a wood,
White blossoms again will spring
And hold sway to hang in full
Above such brooks (though less holy)
As the one being cleansed
On this spot in our time.

# I Have Been Thinking of Late

I have been thinking of late
That the world, though admittedly weary and drawn,
Seems hardly in position
Merely to lie down and die.

Questions, the most critical and profound
Questions, have yet to be answered
Or, in some cases, asked.

And who would want never again to watch
A dazzle of wood ducks land in the marsh
And feed in communion with God?

And there are songs and paintings and poems
Of beauty almost unbearable
Awaiting their creation.

And mankind, poor mankind!
Requires additional time
To learn to distinguish
Between appearance and reality.

# *John Chapman: His Vision*

Singular, questing, nomadic
As an ancient Chinese poet,
Across the lake plains he walked
Attending to his work: Freeing seeds
From the cotton sack slung over his shoulder
And offering them to wind and rain,
The benevolent scatterers,
While he spread the Word to settlers for his supper.
But this creator of orchards was no poet, unless
You see as a poem an apple tree
In starry blossom, or dead, or dying.

# *The Primitive*

October. Time I enter this poem with my pen,
Placing myself in a satiny stand of cherry birch
For observation. The way here follows a wood
Red-leafed, rough, and wild as a trapper's beard.
Not the keenest muzzle trails my fictive scent.

The aged sleeping bear of the Anishinaabe
Stretches across wavy dunes above the deep
Waters of a restive great lake. She knows
Heavy snow windblown like sheets of music
Will cover her hibernal halt. And not till spring
Has this fatted bear been scheduled to eat.

Under a northern skylight tracks will cross
And crisscross the great bear's rank blanket:
Signatures of carcajou, panther, gray wolf,
Creatures driven and derided by hunger
But armed with mangling tools for certain
Slaughter and blood soak in freezing seasons
Stretched and lean. So I begin to sense

The ancient edgy oneness of sentient beings,
Aware that by birthright I too am involved:
I, panting, have often chased the wild game.
And I see as well that when I write, I hunger
And stalk. Relentless I hunger for just words,
Hunt glistening phrases rare as gemstones.

# *Sounding Loon Mountain: Circa 1890*

Hawthorne wrote this country,
Stone height to stern gorge.
Under a face of grey granite, grey
As the old men of this mountain,
In the gloaming I roam struck

By icy time's notched face ticking.
Village lamps burn in low flame;
Shades of red slip-out windows
Of cottages suited to tacit spirits
Suited to deep bonding snows.

So goodwives did gather clandestine
In firelight, dancing 'round totems
Where dark desire flamed in the dark?
Ah, how sins remain cloaked, veiled:
Grave as lime pits slow burning
Or heart sprung sorrow no end.

Out of forest austere past a frisson
Of flume and basin profound (font
Obscure, unfit for sacrament) I am
Confronted by a hard truth: I see
Through a cold frame of pride,

Focused on small cracks in big rocks
And ruts in rugged highland roads.
Surely have I looked with my head
But not with my heart. And now
A darker more sobered soul I must go.

# A Peaceful Day in the Natural World

In the time of autumnal equinox
Cerulean brush strokes create a sky.
Hay bales on tan fields abide in cooling wind,

Stalks of sweet corn rustle to be picked.
A scarlet oak stands like a signal fire
On a knoll of slender grass and round rocks.

A hawk circles aloft, broad-winged, razor-footed;
The brilliant blue jay braced on a branch
Stares. Quarrels. Threatens. Dares.

# A Reckoning

On the matter of faith, I pray
Mine comes short of ostentation,

Seeming fiery enough neither
To burn down another man's hay barn

Nor to roar through seven times seven city blocks.
And surely it does not appear

Wild enough to torch its way
Along grand stretches of cane lands.

Might my faith instead resemble
A campfire whose flame, though it warms

Only a small part of the vast October night,
Clearly is visible from an aerial view.

# *Praise*

I step into a snowy wood
And there they are: iced pine cones
Suspended in moonlight silver
Like holiday bells.

In the silence of winter
I hear them ringing.

# John Proctor Speaks Privately on All Saints' Eve

Times have I entered these dark woods
Where a white moon shines holy,

Where wind makes bare-boned limbs
Thrum like taut harps or lyres attuned,

Where dry leaves rattle in my wake
As if shades claw out of the netherworld;

Where oft is heard the yap of fox
And cry of owl affirming bloodlust.

Yet know I, too, the nightingale's song
That purifies the savage in us all. In truth,

Upon my shadowed forest pathway
Have I met no dusky stranger

Resting on a stone, staff in hand,
Designing to dupe me into perdition.

Such time as this should ne'er be feared;
Of unnatural effects there be none.

# The Railyard in December

Sun rises. Blood thaws.
Seven vigilant doves feather

Down to a lower world,
A cindered world of crosstied steel,

To peck at grain spilled
Out of a boxcar's open door.

It is a feast to them,
It is a kingly feast.

# One Small Hour in Autumn

In time these waters headed westward,
Down off overcut overmined mountains
Then through deep gorges and steep knobs

Into a limestone land of largesse
Where winds bear woodsmoke like incense;
A land of a billion years changing.

I come to search out the shape of insight
In a modest creek that swims slowly
Under an October skylight. I crush

Underfoot wild mint, savor the scent.
Minnows flee to safety, crayfish crawl
Under slate rock. From a mulberry bush

Along the fencerow a hermit thrush sings
Gold in praise of beauty and maroon fruit.
Here children used to play; perhaps no more.

From branches of a blue ash in the blue
Distance, a flock of crows crow
Over coffee after breakfast, full-throated
In mocking my strange inability to fly.

In the pasture five Black Angus focus
And bow to the blessing of dark loam.

O, no more must I shun the inherent
Debt of stewardship to this ground.
I look in the mirror of water, consider

My full reflection; and I begin to think
God, gazing into a similar stream,
Determined final plans for man's image.

Clumps of fallen leaves float past, modeling
Wounded ducks drinking into death:
For the living it's always death and decay

But the stones stay, and this creek flows
Away from and toward, ever away from
And toward all things transit and eternal.

# Ninth Month

Fields greened down.
Barn owls haunting rafters.
Earth fitting herself
Early each morning
With a mask of pale blue
Mystery. A chilling scene.

# *Existential Exercise*

Suppose you heard one night a tapping
Tactful but firm on your door. So
You rose in a fog and answered.
Found standing sublime
On your porch planks a Taoist monk
Who said he had come a long way
In a serious storm. Indeed
His silken robe and wooden flute
Were soaked as stones in the river.

And suppose that, ushering him inside,
You brewed a pot of ginseng tea
And the two of you drank over warm talk
Till he suggested you depart with him
Through the bluestem plains of knowledge
Into the far heights of wisdom.

And further suppose you spurned the offer
After thought brief and shallow as a riffle
And showed him out,
Returned to your eiderdown pillow
And crawled back under your comforter.

Suppose you had chosen *that* different course.

# Go Down in Darkness

The valley runs deep and narrow like an ancient long barrow.
In the first days, the men bored a black hole into the mountain
underworld. They would go in in darkness, go down in darkness,
and come out in darkness. From candlelit shadows on walls
of hollowed caves, they became hewers of magic black
chunks of nascent fire. The slow rain of the ceiling dripped,
dripped, and muddied; the men picked, shoveled, and hauled,
hauled a latent power out of the earth mother and into daylight.
And then they roused those chunks to flicker, flare, and flame
to warm the night sky like a million, million tiny suns. But lo!
the highland sun god did not like to be mocked; thereupon
he charged the depths with choking dust and poisoning air.
The bloodflow of the coal vein dried to a trickle.
The men breathed on, and some sickened, and some died.
Till the able men left the hard valley they had learned to love.
Time passed. They came back; they all came back. And now
they walk the floors and scratch their heads and wait, wait
with a hard-shelled hope while their best selves smother
in the obscure tunnel of old time, while ferns and wildflowers
and greenbriers grow to close wounds in the mountain's side,
while a single star lights the way forward and the way back.

# About the Author

The author of five previous volumes of verse, Steve Holt has been the recipient of the James Still Award for Poetry and an Al Smith Artist Assistance Award, as well as a Pushcart Prize nomination and a nomination for the position of Poet Laureate of Kentucky. Holt taught for many years at the Ohio University Southern Campus, as well as in the Russell (Kentucky) Independent System. He resides in northeast Kentucky by his beloved Ohio River.